coloured for you by:

....

coloured for you by:

....

coloured for you by:

....

coloured for you by:

....

coloured for you by:

....

coloured for you by:

....

coloured for you by:

....

© Rebecca Jones 2017

coloured for you by:

....

© Rebecca Jones 2017

coloured for you by:
....

© Rebecca Jones 2017

coloured for you by:
....

© Rebecca Jones 2017

coloured for you by:

....

© Rebecca Jones 2017

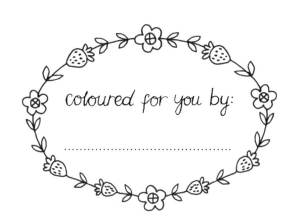

coloured for you by:

....

© Rebecca Jones 2017

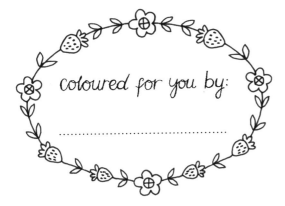

coloured for you by:

....

coloured for you by:

....

coloured for you by:

....

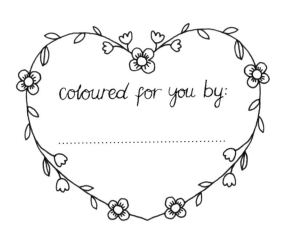

coloured for you by:

....

coloured for you by:

....

coloured for you by:

....

coloured for you by:

....

coloured for you by:

....

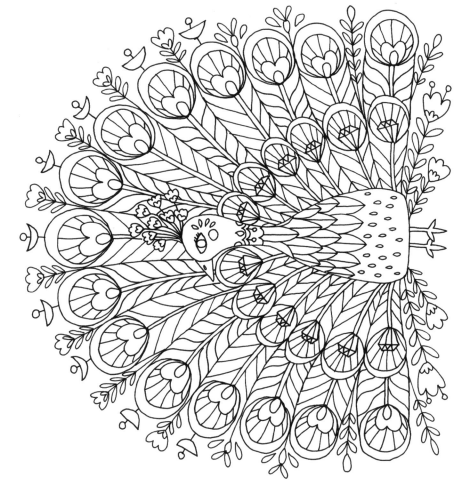

coloured for you by:
....

coloured for you by:
....

Cut carefully along the grey line to neaten the edge of the card. Then snip through the tabs to separate the top card from the bottom card.

Cut carefully along the grey line to neaten the edge of the envelope.

Cut carefully along the grey line to neaten the edge of the envelope.

Cut carefully along the grey line to neaten the edge of the envelope.

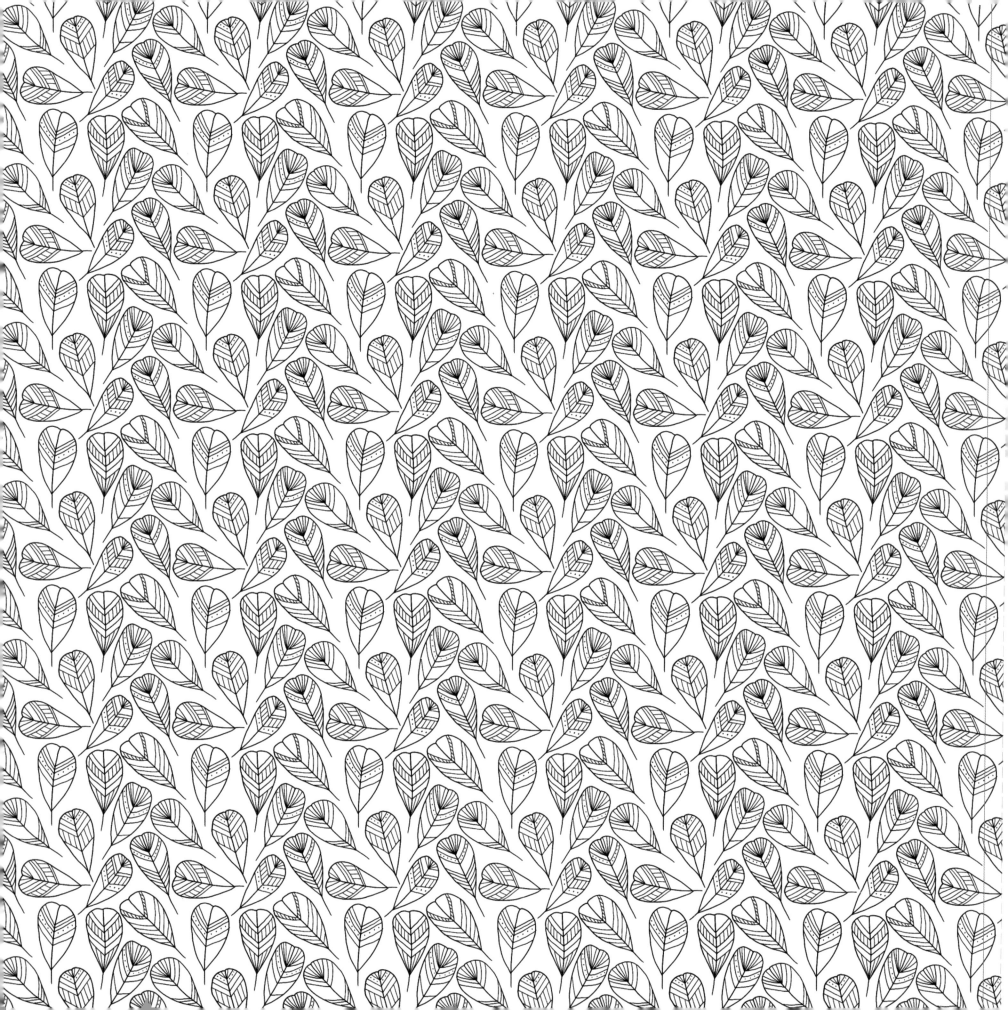

Cut carefully along the grey line to neaten the edge of the envelope.

Cut carefully along the grey line to neaten the edge of the envelope.

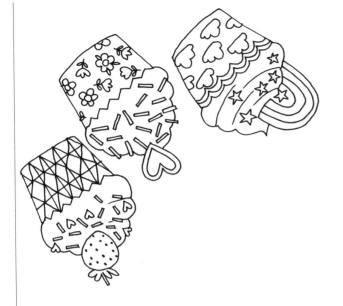

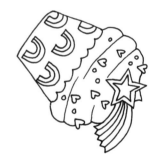

Cut carefully along the grey line to neaten the edge of the envelope.

Cut carefully along the grey line to neaten the edge of the envelope.

Cut carefully along the grey line to neaten the edge of the envelope.

Cut carefully along the grey line to neaten the edge of the envelope.

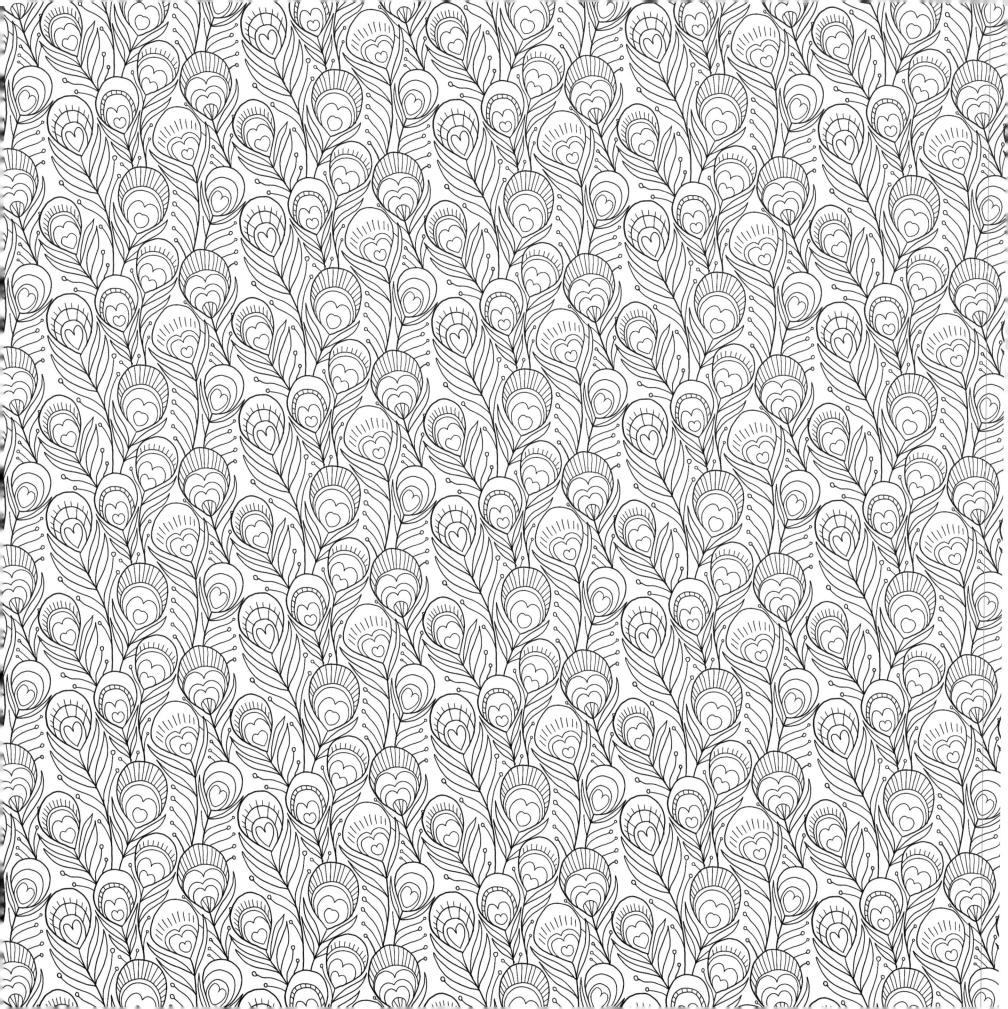

Cut carefully along the grey line to neaten the edge of the envelope.